OKRs, From Mission to Metrics

How Objectives and Key Results Can Help

Your Company Achieve Great Things

Francisco Souza Homem de Mello

OKRs, From Mission to Metrics

How Objectives and Key Results Can Help
Your Company Achieve Great Things

Francisco Souza Homem de Mello

To all my partners in crime at Qulture.Rocks.
Q-Players, you guys Rock!

Contents

CONTENTS

Preface

This is a great time to write about OKRs. I say that because we're at a point of maximum opportunity: there's never been more interest in OKRs, on the one hand, and there's very little understanding of the methodology, on the other hand.

I wrote this book to fill that opportunity gap.

There's no shortage of content around the internet and the bookshelves about the wonders OKRs can do for a company. John Doerr, famed venture capitalist and investor in the likes of Google, has done a terrific job, with his *Measure What Matters*, at selling us how amazing companies can become if they incorporate OKRs in their management routines.

However, managers and entrepreneurs who read these books and, taken by a rush of excitement, decide to implement OKRs in their companies, get very frustrated soon thereafter. That's because reading this stuff makes one conclude OKRs seem simple to implement. That couldn't be further from the truth. OKRs are tricky to implement once you peel its first layer off. And this book aims at solving that.

Our journey

I know how frustrating this journey can be firsthand. When I founded Qulture.Rocks, I had a hunch, which would later be confirmed, that goals must be an integral part of a company's people management toolkit. So we built our product, which goes by the same name, to include goals alongside performance reviews, ongoing feedback and recognition, and one-on-one meetings.

My conviction of the importance of goals logically led to implementing them at Qulture.Rocks - one of our core working principles is to eat our own cooking, sometimes called "dogfooding." Therefore, from the very early days we've intended to use goals to manage the company.

Around the same time, I leraned about OKRs and how they were the answer to all the problems with traditional goal setting, perceived as too complex, bureaucratic, and innefective. So I decided to focus on the OKR "flavour" of goals.

Soon thereafter I became very frustrated: on the one side, questions were mounting on how to unfold OKRs, how to monitor them, how to link them to each other, etc. On the other side, there was very little content online - or offline, for that matter - with which we could answer them. That was in early 2016.

A wave of new content about the subject would infuse us with hope. During the remainder of 2016, then 2017 and 2018, many books and blog posts were written about OKRs. With each announcement, our hopes went up. With each release, they came crashing down. These books and articles were great, but their substance either didn't apply to our reality (because they were written for very small pre-product/market fit startups or agile product teams) or they just lacked sufficient details on the tactics of implementing OKRs throughout an entire organization.

Then came John Doerr's *Measure What Matters*, which I expected would be the definitive guide to OKRs. The book drove an explosion of interest in the subject. I had many fellow entrepreneurs come to me during our Y Combinator batch, book in hand, to tell how great OKRs had to be, since, in Doerr's words, they were the secret behind Google's growth. They also came with many many questions, knowing I was the OKR "expert." The book had made an amazing job at drawing their interest, but left many gaps wide open that would jeopardize an attempt to implement OKRs.

That's about when I decided to write this book. I realized we had to fill that gap and help empower organizations around the world to implement OKRs for real.

In order to write the book, I had to read, basically, everything ever written about OKRs, and then look for the origins of the methodology, that were rooted in Management by Objectives, Hoshin Kanri, and goal-setting theory, or GST.

I read authors like Cristina Wodtke, Ben Lamorte, Paul Niven, John Doerr, Dan Montgomery, Laszlo Bock, and so on and so forth. The list is big. And the feeling of emptyness persisted. There was a lot of cheering OKRs, and very little explaining how a company can run by them on the day to day. But then, I also read the stuff these authors were referrenicing on their books, like books written by Peter Drucker and Andy Grove. And what I found out was that these sources were still pretty perfunctory - they barely scratched the surface. It wasn't enough.

So I dug deeper, and then, finally, struck gold. I found a missing link in authors such as Michelle Bechtell, George Odiorne, Yoki Akao, Vicente Falconi, Thomas Jackson, Randy Kesterson, and Pete Babich. And by looking at these often uncited authors and their works, I found answers to many of the questions that were lingering in my head.

Closing those gaps made all the difference. The symptom

was clear: Using OKRs at Qulture.Rocks became much more fun and effective, and I started to finally feel we were doing a good job at figuring out our strategy and then executing it with excellence.

Why another book about OKRs?

After seeing firsthand how amazing OKRs could be at our own company, I decided to take that knowledge to other companies, and what better way to do that than write a book about the subject?

I had one major goal in writing the book: helping companies implement OKRs. I also knew that our book would probably not be the first contact our readers would have with OKRs. They'd probably get to John Doerr or some other author much faster. So I decided to tackle some of what I understood where conflicting definitions and contradictions found in those authors' works.

These contradictions basically arose from either the poor quality of examples used by authors and sources, such as Google's re:Work website, or by lack of depth in explaining how to actually do it in a company, with various teams, layers of management, etc. Deeper, more relevant examples.

I trully hope you enjoy this book and that it helps your

organization achieve great things.

– Francisco S. Homem de Mello
Founder and CEO, Qulture.Rocks

San Francisco, January 18th, 2019

1. Introduction

"OKRs have helped us on the road to growth many, many times"
–**Larry Page**

"If you do not know where you're going, you probably will not get there"
–**Yogi Berra**

"Vision without execution is just hallucination"
–**Thomas Edison**

OKRs are a powerful management tool that has been gaining ground among innovative companies in the technology, retail and even non-profit sectors. Some of the world's best-known organizations that use it are Google, Dropbox, Twitter, the Gates Foundation, and also more traditional companies like AB Inbev and Disney.

This book works as a practical guide to understand what OKRs are and how to apply them in your company.

What are OKRs?

"OKRs" stands for *Objectives and Key Results*.

OKRs are a tool for guiding and executing the strategy of the organization. They happen through the deployment of business Objectives throughout individuals and teams.

In some respects, they follow the same logic as traditional goals, based on the Balanced Scorecard, Hoshin Kanri, or Management by Objectives, but they have their own agile flavor which makes them more useful to the business challenges of modern companies and professionals.

An OKR is a set of *one* Objective and *n* Key Results.

The Objective is the business result that needs to be achieved, and should be written in qualitative terms.

The Key Results are S.M.A.R.T. (an acronym for specific, measurable, attainable, relevant and time-bound) goals based on specific key performance indicators.

Key Results must help "prove" if the Objective was achieved.

A good OKR should be built in such a way that if the Key Results are all achieved, you should feel comfortable that the Objective has been reached. They must serve as proof of the attainment of the Objective. Alternatively, if you feel that your Objective hasn't quite been achieved even though all Key Results were achieved, there was a problem with your Key Results to start with.

You can use a very simple statement to help form an OKR:

"We will _ _ _ _ _, and we will know if we were successful if we can _ _ _ _ _, _ _ _ _ _, _ _ _ _ _ _."

The first space is filled by your Objective, and the second to the fourth are filled by the Key Results.

Let's use an example to illustrate our definition:

- **Objective**: Increase the profitability of the company
- **Key Results**: i) Grow the company's net income to $100 million, and ii) Reach a net profit margin of more than 7%.

Since OKRs belong to cycles, if they don't have an explicit end date, you must automatically assume that they must be completed before the end of the cycle. Cycles of OKRs generally last 3 months, a period within which the OKRs are established, monitored, and evaluated, and from which a new cycle begins, *ad eternum*.

Back to our example. If we fill in the gaps above, we will have:

"We will *increase the profitability of the company*, and we will know if we were successful if we can *grow the company's net income to $100 million* and *reach a net profit margin of more than 7%*.

Why use OKRs in managing your company?

OKRs are a management tool that brings many great benefits to any company that uses them the right way. Let's see what some of these benefits are:

Focus and prioritization

OKRs force organizations (and teams and individuals) to prioritize the most important business results in a given period (for example, next quarter), and ripple that focus and prioritization throughout the organization.

The focusing effect of OKRs is well documented and researched, especially through the work of American academic Edwin Locke.

Alignment

OKRs come from the company's mission and vision in a process of alignment that has the ultimate goal of getting everyone to know in which direction they should row, here and now.

This alignment process happens in two dimensions: through time and through the organization.

The company creates its strategic OKRs aligned to the mission and the vision. It then creates its annual OKRs aligned to its strategic OKRs. That's aligning them through time.

Within the same cycle, different people and teams within the organization also align their OKRs to each other. VPs create their OKRs in alignment with the company's. Directors create their OKRs in alignment with VPs'. Squads create their OKRs in alignment with the OKRs of business units, and with each other's. That's aligning them through the organization.

The alignment superpower is enhanced by the fact that OKRs are public by default. Dependencies and conflicting OKRs can be promptly identified, discussed, and resolved.

Motivation

It's scientifically proven (again by Locke, long before the term "OKR" existed), that difficult but achievable goals increase task-related motivation.

Because OKRs are less directly linked to employee compensation (i.e., they're a management tool rather than a compensation management tool, which we'll talk more about this later), supporting aggressive goals is encouraged. These goals are called roof-shots, or even moon-shots, depending on how bold they are.

Vicente Falconi, a Brazilian management guru, relates difficult goals to employee engagement when he says that "from the point of view of the people involved, the value of the goal must be above their capacity to reach it, in a way that they need to learn and grow in the process of working towards it."

Culture

OKRs are a very powerful tool for solidifying a culture of execution and results orientation.

Perhaps 9 out of 10 companies have, among their corporate competencies, values, or strategic guidelines, some variation of "results orientation." But what does "results orientation" mean?

In our view, a results-oriented professional clearly knows the difference between an effort and a result. Let's look at some efforts and results that are often confused:

- Attending a sales meeting (or 50, for that matter) is

an effort. Closing sales is a result.
- Implementing an ERP system is an effort. Reducing accounting errors is a result.
- Building a new feature for the e-commerce shopping cart is an effort. Increasing the conversion rate is a result.

The relationship between efforts and results is always relative. To illustrate this, let's think about football. "Running faster" is a result of the "workout" effort, but "running faster" is also an effort to "score more goals." And "scoring more goals" is an effort to "win the game."

An OKRs should track results relative to the person or team that owns them. So, if a product team works exclusively with the shopping cart feature, its Objective will be something like "improve shopping cart conversion rates," and the Key Result will be "improve the conversion rate between adding items to the shopping cart and making a purchase from 3% to 5%."

As people better understand what the results of their efforts are, they create a culture of fewer politics, less subjectivity, and more, *voilá*, results orientation!

Why are OKRs different?

OKRs, in their current application in Silicon Valley, are different than regular goals in the following ways:

- They aren't defined solely top-down: OKRs should be set from both the bottom-up and from the top-down. In practice, employees take a more active role in the process.
- They're less directly linked to variable compensation plans, like pay-for-performance bonuses (we'll talk more about this soon).
- They're run in shorter cycles of 3, 4 or 6 months.
- They're public by default. That means that confidential OKRs are the exception, and not the rule (goals related to mergers and acquisitions or downsizing plans are some examples of private OKRs).

2. A brief history of OKRs

OKRs are goals: old pals from the business world, renamed and tailored to the needs of modern professionals and companies.

It all started with the fathers of management, Taylor and Fayol, who began to face management as a science. They pioneered measuring the times and motions of production line jobs, correlating that to productivity (basically output per unit of input), and then formulating hypotheses about how to improve these results. That's how these guys found out interesting things like the ideal resting time for workers of a given factory, where equipment should be placed around the worker for optimum reach and even better lighting schemes over the production line that minimized the amount of mistakes and waste. In 1916 Fayol was already proposing the use of goals in the management planning process, according to William LaFollette, in his The Historial Antecedents of Management by Objectives, saying that "... in 1916 Henri Fayol identified five functions of management: planning, organizing, command, coordination, and control. Fayol considered the planning function to consist of visualizing the desired end (i.e., the objective or goal), the line of action to be followed, the stages to be followed in sequence, and the methods that would be used. Unfortunately, Fayol's work was unknown in America for some years."

Mace and goal setting

Around 1935, a guy named Cecil Alec Mace conducted the first experiments that would prove that goals improve the performance of workers performing a job.

Mace was born on July 22, 1894, in Norwich, Great Britain. Mace's early passion was theology, and he actually went to Cambridge to enter the holy orders but ended taking up the Moral Sciences. While at Cambridge, Mace took many psychology courses (with mentors and tutors like G.E. Moore, C.S. Meyers, and G.F. Stout), and delved into experimental psychology, a field that would define his career.

In 1935, Mace conducted the first experimental study of goal-setting and in the following years discovered many of the basic principles that are taught today. His findings are absolutely aligned with further discoveries, from Garry Latham and Edwin Locke: first, performance is dependent on the existence of goals. Second, goals can be assigned to individuals, and unless they are too hard to achieve (unrealistic), they will be accepted by said individuals. Third, goals can be assigned for a variety of outcomes: for any performance criterium that can be measured, a goal can be set. Fourth, a tough, specific goal will lead to greater increments in performance than a nonspecific, "do your best" instruction. Fifth, goals increase performance less through intensifying effort than through prolonged effort. And last, despite a worker's internal motivation, without external goal assignment, workers will perform bellow their abilities.

Mace also found out that in order for goals to be effective, individuals need to have constant feedback about their performance in comparison to the goal at hand, and eventual discrepancies.

Since a lot is spoken these days about what motivates individuals at work (the subject of extremely popular books such as Drive, by Daniel Pink, and Payoff, by Dan Ariely), it is very interesting to note that Mace was already reaching very similar conclusions around that time. According to Mace,

> "Traditional doctrine has been oversimple. The mistake of the worldly-wise, who like to say that 'the only effective incentive is the pay-packet', is not so much that they overlook other sources of motivation as that they fail to observe the complexity of this motive itself. We all love money, but we love it most for what it enables us to do. To some, it may mean chiefly beer and circuses, to others it means greater security, or a better chance for one's children, or greater opportunity for

promoting a project for reforming the world. The pay-packet theory is not a bad one to start from, but it is apt to stifle thought precisely at the point where thought should begin."

After Mace's came many studies about the effectiveness of goal-setting in task performance. The subject would be later developed definitively by Locke and Latham, who'd go on to write the bible on the subject.

Peter Drucker, George Odiorne and MBO

In the 1950s, Peter Drucker, who is believed to be the greatest management guru of all time, articulated, in one of his books, that goals could be a great way to measure the performance of managers, a new breed of workers that were popping up left and right on the US economy.

Drucker concluded that managers should set goals around productivity improvements and other measurable outcomes, check performance against those goals from time to time and get on a process of continuous improvement.

He called it "management by objectives and Self-Control", or "MBO", a concept introduced in *The Practice of Management* (Nobody knows who first used the term "MBOs", but it's widely said that it was Drucker. Drucker, on the other hand, actually claims he first heard the term from General Motors's Alfred Sloan).

At the time, one of the most prominent companies to adopt the methodology was HP. Other practitioners included General Mills, DuPont, and General Electric.

Drucker viewed MBO as a management philosophy. According to him, in *The Practice of Management*, "... What the business enterprise needs is a principle of management that will give full scope to individual strength and responsibility, and at the same time give a common direction of vision and effort, establish teamwork and harmonize the goals of the individual with the common weal. The only principle that can do this is management by objectives and self-control."

Contrary to what's currently widely believed, MBO wasn't meant to be top-down nor about controlling people in a mechanistic way. Again according to Drucker, and the emphasis here is mine, "[MBO] **requires each manager to develop and set the objectives of his unit himself**. Higher management must, of course, reserve the power to approve or disapprove these objectives. But their development is part of a manager's responsibility; indeed, it is his first responsibility. **It means, too, that every manager should responsibly participate in the development of the objectives of the higher unit of which he is a part. To "give him a sense of participation" (to use a pet phrase of the "human relations" jargon) is not enough**," and "The greatest advantage of management by objectives is perhaps that **it makes it possible for a manager to control his own performance. Self-control means stronger motivation: a desire to do the best rather than just enough to get by**. It means higher performance goals and broader vision. Even if management by objectives were not necessary to give the enterprise the unity of direction and effort of a management team, it would be necessary to make possible management by self-control.

Drucker's work didn't delve into the specifics of how to apply MBO to an organization. That work was done, in part, by his student pupils, like George Odiorne, who went on to write books about the subject and consult with many large companies in the USA.

Hoshin Kanri, or Policy Deployment, in Japan

Around the 50s, in post-war Japan, W. Edwards Demming and the Japanese manufacturers were developing ways to increase the quality of Japanese products by enhancing their manufacturing processes. Demming had been sent to Japan by the US Government to help rebuild the country's economy, which had been devastated by World War II. That's where methodologies like Six Sigma, TQC – Total Quality Control, and the "Toyota Way" were born.

In Japan, something similar to MBO was developed. It was called Hoshin Kanri, or "policy deployment," a methodology that was part of larger Total Quality Management, and through its process, the goals, or hoshins, were unfolded annually throughout the organization. By the way, we believe that the Hoshin Kanri literature is critical for any company that wants to become an excellent OKR practitioner.

Since the introduction of MBOs and the TQC, practically every modern company is managed using some form of goals. Some companies set annual goals; others do it twice a year. Some tie pay-for-performance bonuses to the achievement of goals; others run some sort of performance review

based on goal attainment. But most of the Fortune 500 use
goals and have them as a key part of their compensation
management stack.

Andy Grove and Intel: iMBOs

The term "OKRs" was coined, as far as is known, by Andy Grove, the western name of András István Gróf, a Hungarian immigrant. Grove was the CEO of Intel for more than 10 years, wrote best-selling business books like *High Output Management* and *Only The Paranoid Survive*, and later taught strategy for high-technology companies at Stanford.

At Intel, goal-management was called "iMBO," or "Intel Management by Objectives" (referring to the term MBO, from Drucker.) Everybody in the office staff took part in it, establishing annual and quarterly Objectives (which resembled SMART goals) and time-bound milestones to achieve those Objectives, which Grove dubbed Key Results. The methodology was taught in an onboarding course though which all those employees went called *Intel's Organization, Philosophy, and Economics*.

Grove didn't bring any transformational insight into the MBO framework but instead suggested that its employees describe their goals (which were basically SMART goals) in conjunction with what they called Key Results, which were steps or action plans that guided the collaborator towards the goal.

In Grove's view, key results were primarily milestones that

would lead someone to achieve their objectives: a goal to "Dominate the mid-range microcomputer component business" would be followed by a key result to "win new designs for the 8085." Even though Grove stressed that key results should be measurable, his examples all closely resemble efforts, or deliverables, as part of an action plan, and don't look like actual results.

Grove's other contribution to OKRs was his belief that Objectives and Key Results should be defined in a two-way process: from top to bottom, in the case of Strategic Objectives that should be deployed to different executives and business units, but also from the bottom up, from the individual contributor herself, so as to bring commitment and empowerment to the process. It was far from a novel concept, but one that had been partially lost in big American companies, which pushed goals "down the line" throughout the organization, from the Board to the CEO, from the CEO to the VPs, and so on. Grove encouraged Intel employees to define their goals according to the goals of the company, and then calibrate them with their managers.

Last but not least, Grove insisted that OKRs were aggressive, meaning difficult to achieve, and what he called "stretch goals."

John Doerr, Google, and OKRs

In the late 1990s, OKRs spread to other Silicon Valley companies through the hands of Jon Doerr, a partner at Kleiner Perkins (now KPCB), one of the world's most respected venture capital firms. Doerr had worked at Intel indirectly under Grove and used iMBOs. He later spread the methodology to some of his portfolio companies at Kleiner Perkins, the most important of which was a startup founded by two Stanford Ph.D. students who had created an excellent web search engine. The startup was Google.

At Google, OKRs took many different forms and gained worldwide fame. Larry Page, a cofounder of Google, claims that "OKRs... helped lead [Google] to 10x growth, many times over. They've helped make [Google's] crazily bold mission of 'organizing the world's information' perhaps even achievable... [OKRs] kept me and the rest of the company on time and on track when it mattered the most."

Google operates under a very loosely standardized flavor of OKRs. Aside from salespeople, who have goals that are set in a more top-down fashion and according to budget, most other teams, like product and engineering, are free to use OKRs or not and use OKRs with varying degrees of homogeneity and effectiveness. In common between all of these flavors, OKRs are treated as more of an HR performance management tool than a management philosophy. They are graded at the end of every performance management cycle in a five-point rating scale (0.0, 0.3, 0.5, 0.7, and 1.0). Laszlo Bock's take on how OKRs should be planned at Google offers a glimpse at why Google users OKRs so loosely:

"Having goals improves performance. Spending hours cascading goals up and down the organization, however, does not. It takes way too much time and it's too hard to make sure all the goals line up. We have a market-based approach, where over time our goals converge because the top OKRs are known and everyone else's OKRs are visible. Teams that are grossly out of alignment stand out and the few major initiatives that touch everyone are easy enough to manage directly."

OKRs have been widely adopted in the Silicon Valley, a phenomenon that can be attributed to Google's fame and success as a company. But there is very little consensus on how OKRs should actually be implemented, or even on what a proper OKR should look like. That's the part of the history of OKRs we'd like to change.

3. A bit of goal-setting science

Goal-setting has historically been used in the corporate world for two main purposes:

- To motivate employees (efficiency)
- To assess their performance

Let me explain this: HR common sense has always said that goals motivate employees towards achieving better results. Goal achievement, on the other hand, has historically been used as a proxy for performance: if I've hit 100% of my goals, it must mean I'm a good performer. However, we thought it made sense to briefly review goal-setting theory or GST. We think HR professionals deserve to have this widespread practice correctly understood from a theoretical basis because there's more to it than just these two axes of purpose.

Goal-setting theory, or GST

According to GST, goals serve three main purposes:

Focus

Presuming that goals have been established according to the company's long, medium, and short-term strategies, based on myriad methodologies like BSC, Hoshin Kanri, etc., goals help the company focus effort, attention, and energy on what's relevant, relative to what's irrelevant. According to Johnson, Chang, and Lord (2006), "goals direct individuals' attention to goal-relevant activities and away from goal-irrelevant activities." It's proven that "individuals cognitively and behaviorally pay more attention to a task that is associated with a goal than to a task that is not."

Effort

Another very important purpose of goals is to increase the level of effort that people exert at work. It's also proven that "goals energize and generate effort toward goal accomplishment. The higher the goal, the more the effort exerted." This is a tricky equation: too hard a goal and, as you'll see in a bit, employees get demotivated; too easy a goal and employees will also get demotivated. In sum, there's a right amount of hard, which pushes people to challenge themselves, but within a reasonable chance of achievement, that optimizes performance. This links us to persistence.

Persistence

Persistence is probably the trickiest thing to get right when setting goals. The right ones produce high effort input for longer periods of time, but the wrong ones can really wreak havoc: "large negative discrepancies may lead to a withdrawal of effort when individuals are discouraged and perceive the low likelihood of future goal attainment" (Carver & Scheier, 1998). As we'll see, there are derivative factors that influence persistence towards goals.

Getting goals right

When GST researches goal efficacy, a lot of attention is given to how individuals relate to their goals, and especially with regard to hitting and not hitting their goals. When there are negative gaps, or when individuals perform below their goals, they seek to attribute the reasons as to why goals haven't been met: "When individuals face negative goal-performance discrepancies, they will likely consider the reasons why they are behind, which systematically determines their subsequent behaviors." Different reasons mean different impacts on how these same individuals take on their future goals: "Attributions, therefore, are an important motivational mechanism that may explain under what circumstances individuals persist in goal pursuit or adjust their goal levels." (By "adjusting their goal levels," you should understand "lowering their goals," or "sandbagging".)

Here's a list of the main attribution mechanisms, and how these may affect future goal-setting:

Internal (self) and external (locus of causality)

If I think I've hit my goals because of my own competence, I'll set harder goals in the future; if I think I've missed my goals because of my own incompetence, I'll try to set easier goals in the future.

Stable and unstable

If I think the reason I've missed my goals isn't going to change (i.e., the reason, or condition, is stable), I'll try to set easier goals, whereas if I think the reason I've missed my goals was a one-off (i.e., not stable,) I'll set higher goals. So, if I think it was due to my lack of effort, it'll be better than if I think it was my lack of competence, which is more stable: "When individuals perceive the cause of the failure or negative goal-performance to be stable and this likely to remain the same in the future, they will likely expect the outcome (i.e., failure to reach their goal) to recur."

Controllable (under the person's control) and uncontrollable

"If people believe that causes for failure are controllable, they will probably continue or renew their effort and commitment to their original goal, but be less likely to do so if the cause of a negative discrepancy or failure is perceived to be due to uncontrollable causes."

Linked to higher goals/purpose

"When making an internal attribution for goal failure, an individual may be more likely to continue goal pursuit when the goal contributes significantly to a highly valued superordinate goal. The individual may be more likely to revise the goal downward when the goal is tangential to the superordinate goal's accomplishment"

Brief bibliographical note

New Developments in Goal Setting and Task Performance, edited by Edwin Locke and Gary Latham, is the most comprehensive piece of science on the effects of goal setting on the performance of people doing jobs. It's a meta-study of more than 500 academic papers and theses on the subject, and it's where we drank most of what's in this chapter. So we won't, for time's sake, be using formal scientific citation formats, because it's 2018 and frankly we don't have time for it. Just remember it all came from them.

4. The current state of goal management

In order to know what proper OKRs look like, we'll first look at how Fortune 500 companies usually do their goals. We'll call that approach to OKRs "Fortune 500 goal management."

First of all, most of these companies manage their goals in an annual cycle, starting and ending in tandem with their fiscal years. At the start of each fiscal year, the company's board sets company-wide goals usually based on financial metrics like revenue growth and profitability.

After company goals have been set, the company starts cascading goals to some of the VPs and business-unit leaders.

In most companies (let's say 90% of them), the cascading process is very limited. These VP and BU goals tend to be further cascaded to those employees and teams who have more measurable results, such as salespeople, and the rest of the company (i.e., whoever's not a salesperson), sets goals for HR purposes, and which feed into performance management, and therefore, compensation. These are the back-office people, like marketing, finance, HR, legal, etc. These HR goals are shallow, of poor quality, and usually mix elements of activities, job descriptions, and projects – stuff like "deliver reports on time," "take excellent care of customers," and "implement the new applicant tracking system." There's usually no KPI behind goals and no distinction between efforts and business results.

Within a second group, which is tiny (let's say 2% of companies) the cascading process is stricter and more centralized. Some companies have a business intelligence team that monitors all corporate KPIs and tends to "own" the goal-setting process, defining target levels for goals and centralizing the planning process. In any case, employees don't know why they have the goals they have. A goal is just something that got pushed onto their lap.

In both types of companies, goal-setting might take from 2 to 4 months of a fiscal year, which leaves less than 20% of the year, at most, for actual work.

Bear in mind that in some companies, goals aren't even touched at the start of the fiscal year. Some of these, due to software rules, will encourage employees to just fill out something on the space reserved for goals. Employees might even just fill everything just with dots and gibberish.

We'll get back to these special companies in a minute. For now, let's focus on the "normal" ones.

By the middle of the fiscal year, HR sets in motion a process of "mid-year goal review," where some employees are allowed to change their goals if external on external factors. It must be noted, though, that revising a goal down, even if that's not going to make it easier because of external, non-controllable factors like the economy, is generally frowned upon. Therefore, most goals are untouched. Also, since goals will lead to compensation down the road, there are usually strict rules around changing goals mid-year.

When the end of the fiscal year starts to roll in, some companies set in motion their performance management ordeal.

As I promised you, we need to make an appendix and go back to those companies where employees filled *dot dot dot* on their goals. Now is the time when these people will log into the system and fill in their goals for the year, just in time for performance reviews. Obviously, quality is terrible, and goals are treated as mandatory pain.

So performance reviews may start with a self-review, where the employee rates the attainment of each of her goals on a scale of 1 to 5 or something. There's maybe a 360-degree component that follows, where employees will get "feedback" from peers and direct reports. Finally, managers log in and review those goals, using the same 1 to 5 rating system, overwriting employee's self-reviews.

After these manager ratings are set, companies may engage in calibration sessions where employees are stack-ranked against each other and have their ratings changed to fit an ideal statistical distribution. At GE, until the early 2010s, for example, ratings had to be massaged so that only 20% of the employees got the highest ratings, 70% got the middle ratings (like 2, 3, and 4), and 10% necessarily got the lowest grades (and ended up fired.)

Another complication is when companies create rules where goal attainment is directly fed into compensation decisions. At these organizations, for example, if an employee reaches 65% of his goals (a weighted average may be used), she earns a bonus equivalent to 3 monthly salaries, whereas an employee who reaches 90% of her goals may earn 6 monthly salaries as pay-for-performance. These systems front-load significant pressure and tension, driving employees and managers to politically negotiate easy goals so as to maximize their chances of good bonuses down the line.

For further complication, goals aren't the only "axis" under which employees are rated. Some companies also rate people on behaviors, which might be dubbed "competencies," "values" or even "culture fit." If an employee has fared badly on her goals but put in the effort, is in managers' good graces, or if she's regarded as a high-potential employee, the behavior part of the review might be bumped up to compensate for poor goal attainment.

At some point, which can happen after the end of the fiscal year, managers and their direct reports sit down to go over ratings and possible compensation changes and promotions, and a new cycle is born.

Now let's talk about how OKRs are different from Fortune 500 goal management.

5. What's different in OKRs

OKRs are goals. So why all the fuzz? Great point. OKRs are an adaptation of the traditional practice of MBOs suited to the more unstable and competitive reality of today's companies. The purpose of this chapter is to explain the main differences between what you see Fortune 500 companies doing and what we know as OKRs.

In many respects, a well-done practice of OKRs closely resembles what one reads in Total Quality books from the 80s and 90s, like those from Michele Bechtell and Pete Babich. However, most big companies have disfigured the practice and hijacked it for compensation purposes. We believe that's the root of all of what's wrong with goals.

Compensation

The main difference between OKRs and Fortune 500 goal management is the degree of linkage between goal attainment and employee compensation. When this link is broken, a number of possibilities open up that make goal management much more effective and engaging.

In these organizations, how much of a goal is achieved is the basis for employee variable compensation, known as "pay-for-performance." If she reaches 100% of her goals, she makes Y times her monthly/yearly salary.

Some companies may even mingle this formula with corporate-level goal triggers, which can increase or decrease distribution. In these cases, nobody may earn bonuses if the company doesn't reach, for example, 70% of the EBITDA goal. Other companies may also factor in team-level compensation so that the employee is encouraged to cooperate with her teammates while reaching her goals.

One of the problems with that is that it can lead to an effect called *sandbagging*: employees tend to whine to managers and schmooze up to them to negotiate easier goals, so they can have a better chance of reaching them.

It also leads to ethical problems like what happened to

Wells Fargo and its executives, who were opening fake accounts in the name of customers and "selling" these customers products they had goals on.

With OKRs, the percentage of achievement of an Objective or its Key Results doesn't matter that much. The actual results achieved are what's important, or the numerator. In Fortune 500 goals, the quotient (percentage of completion of a goal) is what matters, as a proxy for the results achieved.

All the following differences, which can be counted as OKR advantages, derive from this partial detangling of OKRs and compensation.

What about meritocracy?

It must be noted that the fact that goal-attainment isn't directly used as a proxy for performance, and thus pay-for-performance schemes, doesn't mean companies that use OKRs are less meritocratic. Quite the contrary can be possible.

Employee's careers should still be advanced based on merit. Great performers should still be directed to the bulk of the companies' scarce resources, like money, opportunities, and challenges. But the process of allocating these resources won't be derived from a simple mathematical formula (like if you reach x% of your goal you make y% of salary as a bonus,) which encourages sandbagging, unethical behavior, and excessive complexity. Bonuses and other forms of incentives will be derived from manager discretion based on a lot of deep, meaningful discussions, and on the actual results achieved.

Short cycles and nested cadences

At its most fundamental level, OKRs are set and reset in shorter cycles, ranging from 1 to 6 months, while the traditional goals tend to be run on annual cycles. OKRs also work on nested cadences: As you'll see, the short cycle, which is the fundamental unit of OKR management, ranges from 1 to 6 months, depending on the maturity of the business and the practice. These short cycles are nested into an annual cycle, which is nestled into a strategic cycle (from 3 to 10 years), which is nestled into the company's mission and vision. Just like Russian dolls.

Transparency

OKRs are public by default. That means the great majority of individual and team OKRs will be open for consultation by anyone in the company. Exceptions apply to confidential stuff like mergers, cost reduction plans that may imply layoffs, etc.

Transparency leads to more alignment and commitment towards the goals. Alignment because people can resolve conflicts and dependencies faster. Commitment because people know how their work impacts the bigger picture.

Bottom-up and top-down

OKRs are set in a more decentralized way, giving more voice and participation to teams and their members.

In Fortune 500 goal management, goals can be deployed from the top-down in a formal and rigid way, by strategic planning or business intelligence team. People have no say in the process and therefore may feel much less committed to goals that were set for them.

OKRs, on the other hand, are more engaging: employees are encouraged to set their OKRs themselves in line with other, higher goals (such as their team's or the company's), and then discuss them with managers for cohesion and alignment.

But beware: That doesn't mean the process should be chaotic or unsynchronized. Alignment is of the utmost importance and should be a primary goal of the process. People need to row in the same direction, so having a more bottom-up process doesn't mean that people can set their goals however they want or pick projects without reasoning.

Moonshots

This is a polemic topic.

Google defends that OKRs be set very aggressively so that hitting 70% of them takes a lot of effort. They say that if you're reaching all 100% on your goals (or 1s – we'll see more about Google's OKR grading system shortly,) they're too easy. They also say some of your goals have to be even more aggressive, what they call "moonshots."

We think the "70% x 100%" discussion is about semantics. If 70% means "achieved with effort," it basically becomes the new 100%, and people will just adjust to that.

Anyway, what matters is that when OKRs are set with less of a link to compensation, they can also be set more aggressively, which, as proven by Locke and Lathan (we saw that earlier), leads to better performance under other conditions (like these goals being achievable and the "owners" feeling committed to them). The idea is that if the company as a whole aims a bit higher, it will achieve better results.

6. OKRs and strategy

"One day Alice came to a fork in the road and saw
a Cheshire cat in a tree. 'Which road do I take?' she
asked. 'Where do you want to go?' was his response.
'I don't know,' Alice answered. "Then," said the cat,
'it doesn't matter!'"
-**Lewis Carroll**, Alice in Wonderland

Multiyear strategic planning may seem like a joke in today's fast-paced business world. It seems that we can't
even plan 6 or 8 months ahead – but can we operate without a plan? A North Star? We think some kind of plan is still
essential, a plan against which decisions can be made. And
we think OKRs can be a key component of that plan.

Our strategic planning framework starts with inspirational
mission and vision statements, which are then translated
into 3 or 5-year strategic OKRs (which can be referred to
as a "dream," or as Jim Collins says, a "Big, Hairy, Auda-
cious Goal"), annual OKRs and finally 1- to 6-month OKRs,
which we call the short cycle. Let's get that straight:

- Vision: The company has a missionary/visionary goal, which takes several years to be achieved. At Qulture.Rocks, our vision is "a world where all companies have incredible cultures."
- Strategic OKRs: Here the OKRs can be quite "hairy" but with measurable contours (and can even be formatted as actual OKRs). From the vision, which is more inspiring and qualitative, we try to derive metrics that may prove, for example, 10 years from now, if we're on the right track. At Qulture.Rocks, our 5-year OKR is "to increase our impact globally," and its Key Results are "more than 1 million people using our products and services" and "users in over 10 countries." They'll help us gauge if we're on the right track to reaching our vision.
- Annual OKRs: Based on 3- to 5-year goals, the company sets annual corporate goals, which must be communicated by the CEO to the entire company at the beginning of each fiscal year. In the case of Qulture.Rocks, we have a revenue growth target.
- Short-cycle OKRs: Finally, the company, teams, and employees set their short-cycle OKRs in 3-month cycles.

Vision and mission

vi · sion (/ viZH◼n /) noun: The ability to think or plan the future with imagination or wisdom; a mental picture of what the future will or could be.
–Google Dictionary

"If people do not internalize the organization's mission and vision, they will not use them to make day-to-day decisions, and if they do not use them in their daily lives, all the effort will have been in vain."
–Pete Babich

At Qulture.Rocks we read many Silicon Valley pundits talking about mission and vision statements and are amazed by how little clarity and how much confusion there is around what these terms really mean, why they exist, and how companies can leverage them the most. Therefore, we're going to talk a bit about how to write your company's mission and vision statements.

How pundits define mission and vision

Pundits (a general term for whoever tries to define these terms) rarely agree on what a great mission or vision statement really means.

To start, let's look at one of the most referred to articles on the subject: Jim Collins' "Building Your Company's Vision," which went on to become the core idea behind *Good to Great*, Collins' business best-seller.

In the first line of the article, which was published in the Harvard Business Review, Collins and his co-author, Jerry Porras, write "Companies that enjoy enduring success have a core purpose and core values that remain fixed while their strategies and practices endlessly adapt to a changing world." Reading that is already very confusing. In an article about vision, the author has a first-line talking about core purpose and core values.

They then try to clarify it a bit, and go on to say "[vision] has two principal parts: core ideology and envisioned future."

Let's examine this a bit more.

By Googling "how to build company vision," we stumble upon an article at the Openview Venture Partners website, written by portfolio CEO Firas Raouf, that defines mission as "what a company is striving to be in the long term" and vision as "how it can get there," asking "what things need to be executed to accomplish the mission?"

How big companies write their mission and vision

Companies' websites don't really help us better understand what these concepts – mission and vision – mean.

Google's mission statement, found on its website, is "… to organize the world's information and make it universally accessible and useful." There's no mention of there being a vision. If we unpack it, there's a first part that talks about how Google makes an impact on the world (organizing the world's information and making it easier to retrieve). Then, there's a part that talks about how Google wants the world to look (a world where information is organized and universally accessible and useful).

On the other hand, Amazon's mission statement is "to be Earth's most customer-centric company, where customers can find and discover anything they might want to buy online, and endeavor to offer its customers the lowest possible prices." Amazon's mission concentrates on what the company wants to become (Earth's most customer-centric company). It goes on to explain in more detail how that'll be true (where customers can find a lot of stuff cheaply).

It seems like these two giants don't define their vision

statements. They only talk about their missions. Now, if we read their missions, it's very hard to abstract a consistent pattern on what a mission should look like.

In the "old economy"

If we look at the "old economy" for reference, we get even more confused. Koch Industries, for example, defines its vision as: "Koch Industries is a trading, investment and operating company that aggressively identifies and acquires companies in which it can leverage our strengths to generate superior earnings or market value." Their mission is "Koch Industries seeks to maximize the present value of future profits. Doing so provides security and opportunity for stockholders and productive employees, while also benefiting customers and society...."

Now, unpacking Koch's mission and vision is a trip. Their mission basically describes what business the company is in (buying out other companies for cheap). Their vision, on the other hand, describes what benefit the company wants to bring to its stakeholders (security and opportunity for stockholders and employees, and less explicit benefits to customers and society).

Our definition

If you're feeling more confused than when you started reading this article, that's exactly how we felt when we tried to understand what great mission and vision statements look like to articulate our own statements at Qulture.Rocks.

After this long journey, which included countless other references, we agreed upon the following definition:

The mission is the company's purpose. It's why it exists. A great helper is to think "How would the world be negatively impacted if our company ceased to exist?" At Qulture.Rocks, for example, our mission is to "help people and organizations achieve great things through great cultures and growth."

The vision is how the world will look like if the company fulfills its purpose. At Qulture.Rocks, our vision is "a world where everybody can work at a culture that rocks."

As you can see, mission and vision statements are like two sides of the same coin. If the company fulfills its mission, the world will look like its vision. If it reaches its vision, it will have fulfilled its mission. So if they're well written, both statements will feel harmonious.

Company-centric x customer-centric

Using broad strokes, the company's mission can be company-centric or customer-centric. Google's mission (or the part of it that looks like a mission by our definition) is customer-centric. If a customer reads it, she immediately relates the company's impact on her own life. Koch's mission, on the other hand, is company-centric. It basically talks about how the company makes money in very practical terms.

We believe missions should be as customer-centric as possible, and abstract in nature. At Qulture.Rocks, for example, we're not talking about anything other than the impact we were created to have on the world.

Another good guideline is to not mention your line of business in your mission and vision statements. They should be more about the world, and less about the how of your company's impact. The how is more about strategy and tactics: how the company chooses, today, to bring that impact to the world. However, that can change if it ceases to be the most efficient way to do it.

For example, we don't cite software or technology in our mission statement. That's because we're about cultures that rock, and not about software. Software is how we choose to pursue our mission, but it can change to another thing (content, consulting, wearables) if we think that would cause more impact.

Back to Google and Amazon

Now that we've – hopefully – agreed on the definition of a mission and vision statements, let's go back to Amazon's and Google's mission statements and see how they pass our test.

Again, Google's mission statement is "to organize the world's information and make it universally accessible and useful." It's kind of a blend between a mission and a vision. The first part looks like a mission: Google exists to organize the world's information and make it easy to access. However, it gradually blends into a vision, because it gives us a vivid description of what the world will look like if they're successful: a world where all information is easy to access and useful. We'd give it a 7.

Amazon, on the other hand, has a worse mission statement. As we saw earlier, it reads "to be Earth's most customer-centric company, where customers can find and discover anything they might want to buy online, and endeavors to offer its customers the lowest possible prices." That looks much more like a vision statement to us, and quite a company-centric one, for that matter. It describes a future, but in terms of what the company will look like in the future, and not how the world will look.

Recap

By now, I hope you have a better grasp of what constitutes good mission and vision statements. As we've seen, a mission is the company's purpose. It's why it exists. A great helper is to think "how would the world be negatively impacted if our company ceased to exist?" Vision is how the world will look like if the company fulfills its purpose. Your company doesn't need to talk about both a mission and a vision. As we've also seen, when they're well-written, they kind of convey the same message to readers. Google's, for example, is a mission statement with elements of a vision statement and that's fine. Just make sure people can understand, in terms that are relevant to them, why your company exists and/or how the world will look if it fulfills its purpose.

Strategic OKRs

From the vision and mission of the company, which are quite generic in terms of how they can be achieved, the next step is to define your strategy. Some aspects of company strategy are usually already defined in the present, such as the geographic market in which it operates, the nature of the products and services it offers customers, and so on. The hard part of a company's strategy is to make decisions about how these variables should change in the future so that the company gets closer to its vision.

A good strategy is usually painful to produce because it forces the company to make difficult choices (or trade-offs). It's impossible to compete for price and quality at the same time. It's difficult to be in all markets at once. Resources are scarce and certain choices make other choices unfeasible. Some of the variables that make up a company's strategy are:

- Competition for cost/price or differentiation: The most basic aspect of a company's strategy is to choose one of two major paths identified by Michael Porter, a Harvard scholar. In most markets, the same product can't, in a sustainable way, compete for price and quality. Bear in mind that some offerings may provide both for some time in order to quickly rob market share – but it can often be unsustainable.

- Geography: The company has to choose where it will operate. Certain businesses are easier to expand nationally or internationally. A company may want to dominate one market before expanding into another, while another company may want to "plant its flag" in a large number of markets, albeit without attaining the dominance of any of them. In addition, in some industries or sectors, leaders can focus more on returns (profits), while others may concentrate on them less.

- Portfolio of products and services: The company has to choose what products and services to offer. One option is to focus on one or a few products, making them very complete (a vertical approach). Another is to expand its offerings horizontally, having many shallower products.

- Customers: The company has to choose how it will serve its customers. This is necessary whether focusing on a specific customer niche, addressing its needs in a very deep way, or focusing on a broad group of customers and serving its needs in a shallower way.

- Organic growth or acquisitions: The company has to choose which will be its main growth generator: whether it will grow organically – that is, by investing in its own operations (as most startups grow) – or through acquisitions and possible incorporation of other products and businesses (as most large high-growth companies grow).

The strategic decisions of a company, some of which we discussed above, should be quantified by strategic OKRs.

No need to panic

Don't despair if you don't know exactly what your organization's vision, mission, or strategy are. You don't need them in order to start setting OKRs. Keep it simple.

What's important is that these things start being discussed and eventually decided. They'll make running your company, and focusing on the right things, much easier.

Something that should make your life easier: 99% of companies should have visions that are based on maximizing the organization's impact in the world through the mission. We believe that any successful company has to have growth as its major objective, and this objective already works very well as a guideline for strategic and annual OKRs.

Growth is key to the success of any business.

From strategy to strategic OKRs

As we've seen, strategic OKRs unfold from the company's mission, vision, and strategy.

These OKRs are a way for the company to articulate its strategy into actions (Objectives) and establish metrics that will prove whether or not the strategy is being executed (Key Results). Strategic OKRs:

- Cover long terms, between 3 and 10 years
- Must be revised annually
- Quantify the path to the vision of the company
- Must be constantly communicated within the organization (the main job of a CEO)

From these strategic OKRs, we begin to enter into the world of "what" and "how." What do we have to do to reach our strategic OKRs? What are the critical gaps that we need to close to get there?

Annual OKRs are born from strategic OKRs in the same manner.

Annual OKRs

From the strategic OKRs, which cover 3 to 10 years in the future, the company must set its annual OKRs at the start of its fiscal year.

A great way to structure your company's annual OKRs is through the Balanced Scorecard lens.

The theory, created by Robert Kaplan and David Norton, defines that a company must measure its success in balanced, sustainable ways. A company can't prioritize its financial results (profit margins, revenues, and earnings per share) if that means jeopardizing customer or employee experience. In addition, the company can't prioritize only its financial results, which are usually measured in the short term, to the detriment of its long-term competitiveness. Thus, financial results, long-term sustainability, customer, and employee needs must be "balanced."

If we're to define the company's annual OKRs in a "balanced" way, we'll generally have three main objectives: one related to financial and business results; one related to customer satisfaction; and finally, one related to the employee experience. Let's see an example:

Objective 1: Grow revenue with profitability

Key Result 1.1: Net revenue of $12 million

Key Result 1.2: Net margin of 12%

Objective 2: Become a company loved by our employees

Key Result 2.1: Improve employee engagement rate by 20%

Key Result 2.2: Reduce company turnover by 25%

Objective 3: Enchant our customers

Key Result 3.1: NPS of at least 50% in all our products and services

Key Result 3.2: Reduce the number of complaints to 20 per day per customer

In companies where annual OKRs suffice, everything we'll talk about hereafter can be applied to the annual cycle. That is, in these companies we can ignore the annual OKRs as a distinct step from short-cycle OKRs.

We do believe, though, that these days almost no company can abstain from having at least a 6-month short cycle within its fiscal year. Business is just too competitive and fast-paced for that. So make that choice at your own risk.

7. The OKR short cycle

Great. Now that we've talked a lot about the more strategic and long-term aspects of OKRs, let's get down to business and talk about how OKRs are run day-to-day. We're talking about the short OKR cycles: the heart of the methodology.

Nested cadences, or cycles

As we saw earlier, OKRs are run on nestled cadences or cycles.

Any company operates simultaneously in at least four cycles: the mission/vision, which have no expiration date; the strategic OKRs, which can cover from 3 to 10 years; the annual OKRs, which generally operate in parallel with the company's fiscal and budgeting cycles; and finally, the short cycle OKRs, which have terms ranging from 1 to 6 months.

Over time, the company will be conducting its short cycles, which in the quarterly example are four within the annual cycle, and so on, as we can see in the image below:

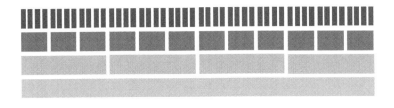

OKR's Nested Cycles

Of course, in the first cycle, the company can make an extra effort if it doesn't already have its mission/vision, strategic, and annual OKRs set before it can set its quarterly OKRs. However, as we saw earlier, don't panic: you don't need to get them set all at once.

Figuring out the mission, vision, and strategy can take time, so the company may choose to run a few short cycles before determining that stuff. What's important is that it eventually gets discussed: If you don't know where you're going, anywhere will do.

Fortune 500 goal management doesn't have a short cycle. Only an annual, fiscal-year cycle is done, possibly coupled with a Pro-forma mid-year review.

One of the great advantages of OKRs is, as we've seen, the increased speed with which the company and its employees course-correct and respond to the market and innovation. Therefore, it makes sense that you implement some short-cycle variation in your company, even if it is semiannual.

The short cycle

The size of a short OKR cycle, which is contained within the annual cycle, can vary based on various factors, such as the stage and strategy of the company and its market. Companies in more fast-paced, undefined markets (let's think ridesharing) can do monthly, bimonthly or quarterly cycles. Companies in more stable markets, or with more established businesses, can perform quarterly or semiannual cycles.

It's important to note that short cycles are where the magic of OKRs happens.

Short cycles have 3 phases:

- Planning
- Monitoring
- Debriefing

Planning is where OKRs are set throughout the company.

The first step is setting the company OKRs. The second step is having teams and persons create their OKRs in alignment with the company's and with each other.

The third step is as important as the first two: OKR owners have to plan how they'll reach their OKRs by deciding on a hypothesis, as well as planning actions that will be taken to try that hypothesis out. The process is similar to what's done on a Lean Startup.

The company then goes into monitoring mode. Here, the aim is to track metrics on which the Key Results were based and action plans/initiatives that were planned. If the plan is being executed and the Key Result is moving closer to the target, that's a best-case scenario. We'll get into that later.

Finally, the cycle ends with a debriefing of the results achieved, which kicks off a new cycle and its planning (often concomitantly).

In the next chapters, we'll look at each step of the short cycle in detail.

8. Planning

"Vicente Falconi gave us goal-setting, which is the most important thing. It is useless having company goals that don't unfold to everybody. That you can and need to do better – and then deploy it to the whole enterprise. It makes you unbeatable, a machine."

- **Marcel Telles**, board member, Anheuser Busch Inbev, Kraft Heinz and Restaurant Brands International

Unfolding or deploying OKRs is the first pillar of the planning phase. It's the process of transforming the organization's Objectives – which are, by definition, the CEO's Objectives – into Objectives, Key Results, Projects, and Action Plans for the entire company.

One of the great benefits of OKRs and goals, in general, is ther effectiveness as a means of translating organizational strategy down to everybody's reality, so that the whole organization becomes aligned and focused on what matters most. They become true north for the whole organization to guide and prioritize its efforts.

Imagine there's no such alignment: The CEO and the board define that the priority of the year is to grow market share in an organic way to defend the company's position against potential Chinese competitors. However, this priority isn't well-communicated to the organization, so after six months, operations are focusing on margins, to the detriment of growth (trade-offs, again); others are looking at new disruptive technologies; corporate development is trying to map M&A opportunities. All the power of the organization is lost over a lack of clarity regarding what are the *real* priorities.

With OKRs, the company strategy is reduced very simply to one or more pairs of Objectives and Key Results. As everyone in the organization knows the OKRs of the company, they can define their OKRs accordingly, so that – in the words of Jorge Paulo Lemann, founder of the brewery which has now become AB Inbev, the world's largest – they all "row in the same direction."

A controversial point is how this unfolding process (that is, the mechanics of transforming CEO OKRs into OKRs for the company's teams and individuals must happen.

To cascade or not to cascade? That is the question

> "Having goals improves performance. We have a market-based approach, where over time our goals converge because the top OKRs are known and everyone else's OKRs are visible. Teams that are grossly out of alignment stand out, and the few major initiatives that touch are easy enough to manage directly. "

–**Laszlo Bock**, former VP People Operations, Google

The vast majority of OKR experts argue that there should be no formal, centralized goal-setting process across the organization.

Google's former VP of People Operations, Laszlo Bock, said that 60% of targets must be set from the bottom up, that is, by the employees in conjunction with their managers. In this model, it's up to the employees and their managers to set aligned OKRs without any formal control of the process. In more traditional organizations, such as AB InBev, which derive their management by guidelines from the traditional Japanese, Hoshin Kanri model, the process tends to be much more centralized and "top-down." There is little room for an employee to question the goals assigned to her, performed by a centralized "management" function which does a meticulous work of unfolding goals and tracking KPIs, and that can last up to 4 months.

Ignore "Google"

As one of the best-known companies in the world and because it's often cited as a pioneer in adopting OKRs, Google is always held as a benchmark in content and methodology for OKRs.

Our suggestion is that you ignore any reference to Google in implementing your OKRs. First of all, things that work for Google might not necessarily work for your company. Second, our empirical research with more than 20 Google employees has shown that there's no homogeneous format for OKRs within the company, or between departments (e.g., how sales or product treats the subject) or across geographies (e.g., how Brazil, the US, and Europe address the issue). We've even found that four of those people that didn't even know what OKRs were, and many who used OKRs as a high-level task list, which it's NOT.

Some official Google resources on OKRs, such as their human resources website, *re:Work*, explain the methodology simplistically and give out terrible OKR examples (one suggested Objective is "Eat 5 Pies").

Finally, don't learn about management from companies that don't really need to be well-managed. Google is a money minting machine because of its Adwords advertising business, and it really doesn't matter if it has a strategy or not, or how well it executes it: Cash will keep pouring in. For execution lessons, look at tougher businesses, like retail and manufacturing. That's where management really can make or break a company.

Obviously, there are pros and cons inherent in both the fully centralized and the fully decentralized deployment models: On the one hand, the more decentralized the unfolding process, the less precise it tends to be, so that adding up people's contributions may not result in achieving corporate goals and strategy. On the other hand, a more decentralized process is faster and forces the organization to internally communicate all the context necessary for the setting of "bottom-up" OKRs (that's why several companies share their results presentations from their Board of Directors with all of their employees, in an "all-hands" meeting).

A more centralized process can be quite precise but slow

and not very engaging to employees (so much so that traditional organizations attach large variable compensation
packages to goal attainment). For companies where the
workforce is composed mostly of creative professionals
– Google calls them smart creatives – a more decentralized process may be better. For manufacturing companies
that produce very stable, low-tech products, and where
the workforce is composed, in large part, by blue-collar
professionals, centralized goal-setting and planning can
make more sense.

Let's compromise

In our view, all OKRs have to be well-aligned. Everybody
has to row in the same direction. That's the biggest advantage of OKRs.

How the alignment should happen is the million-dollar
question. We think doing it top-down, and not engaging
people in the process is a waste of time and gray matter.
People should know why the company has the direction
it has, and actively think through the unfolding process.
That's because a lot of the benefits of OKRs accrue from
having people burn neurons thinking about how they can
contribute to greater goals and to the company strategy.
The quality of the alignment must be an important principle of the process.

Some OKRs will tend to be deployed in a more top-down fashion. Sales quotas, for example, and financial metrics have little room for negotiation. People just have to make them. (Of course, it's crucial to explain to people *why* these targets are important for the company. Without a why, people won't feel motivated to hit them without heavy external incentives, like cash.) In other areas, such as product and marketing, there will be more leeway in defining what Objectives will be achieved and how to measure their completion through Key Results.

But the most engaging part of the planning process should be having people figure out *how* they'll achieve their OKRs.

OKRs have to be aggressive enough so that people don't quite know how to reach them at the start of the journey. Even if they have an idea of what they should do, there must be a chance of the OKR not being hit.

For example, let's say your company needs to grow 25% in revenues in a given quarter. How the company will hit that goal is going to be a matter of great thinking and creativity. The journey starts with analyzing the data to understand pockets of opportunity. Where can the sales process be improved? Where is there breakage in the sales process? Where are the low hanging fruits? Let's say this analysis shows that salespeople have too few leads and therefore need more leads to work on. You then calculate that at your recent-past conversion rates, you'd need to grow leads by 100% in order to grow sales by 25%. That's the first hypothesis. So you unfold a "grow the number of leads" Objective to marketing and a Key Result of "generate 15,000 more inbound leads quarter-on-quarter." Of course, there's a chance that growing leads won't result in more sales. Getting it right is good management and good thinking.

But moving further, how to grow leads is also going to be based on a hypothesis. We can plan to release three e-books and 10 webinars during the quarter, and they can close the 15,000 lead gap. Or not. Releasing three e-books and 10 webinars become the action plan for the "grow leads" OKR. That's how the planning process should work, and it needs to engage people's brains in order to be successful.

It really makes little sense that most companies stop to centrally deploy goals to 100% of employees, a process that, when very agile, can take more than two months of sweat. This whole effort might even make sense in an annual cycle, but it's totally crazy to spend 50% of a three-month short cycle on planning.

We also think that if the discussion process of unfolding and aligning OKRs is well done, the alignment will be an inevitable consequence. VPs will align their goals with those of the CEO; directors with those of their VPs, and so on. If there's no immediate linkage of goals to remuneration, believe me, this conversation becomes productive and enriching for the whole company, rather than a political give-and-take negotiation.

Unfolding and aligning OKRs

The planning stage of OKRs is composed mainly by the process of unfolding the Goals (and Projects) through the organization, then assigning Key Results to each Objective, and determining hypotheses and action plans to reach them.

Now let's talk a bit about the technique of unfolding and aligning OKRs. Then we'll give you a blueprint on how to conduct this process in your company.

Unfolding Objectives

The first step in unfolding OKRs in your organization is to unfold the Objectives. This process always begins with the organization's Objectives, which are usually the same as the CEO's. As we break down the company OKRs into other OKRs, Projects and Action Plans, we understand what each and everyone in the organization has to do (and how the results of their efforts will be measured) for the company to get where it needs to go.

Unfolding an Objective is the process of filling in the following gaps:

"In order to _ _ _ _ _ , we will have to_ _ _ _ _ _ ,
_ _ _ _ _ _, and _ _ _ _ _"

In the sentence above, the first space is filled by the Objective to be unfolded (remember, we always start with the organization's Objectives), and the following ones are filled by the new Objectives and Projects that will enable us to hit the original Objective.

Let's use an example to illustrate our definition:

- **Objective to be unfolded**: Increase the profitability of the company
- **Objectives unfolded**: Increase sales; Cut costs and expenses; Implement Six Sigma

Therefore, if we fill in the gaps of the previous sentence, we'll have:

"In order to *increase the profitability of the company*, we will have to *increase sales, cut costs and expenses* and *implement Six Sigma.*"

In this case, our original Objective ("increase the profitability of the company") gave rise to two other Objectives ("increase sales" and "cut costs and expenses") that, if realized, will contribute to the fulfillment of the original

Objective. The Objective also gave rise to a Project based on a hypothesis that "Implementing Six Sigma" will help increase the profitability of the company. This process repeats itself until Objectives can no longer be deployed, and become action plans to be performed by someone (or a group). Remember: All Objectives have to become Action Plans and Projects to be executed. If they don't, nothing is going to change. Change happens through effort, that may – or may not – lead to results. And OKRs must measure results.

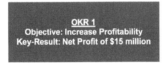

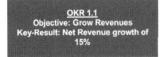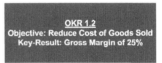

Unfolding an Objective into different Objectives

Sometimes we don't break an Objective into different constituents. In these cases, we repeat the Objectives and change only the measurement scope or the KPI on which Key Results are based. Basically, the Objective remains the same when it's unfolded and only Key Results change (we'll see this later in more depth). This kind of unfolding works very well, for example, for sales: Imagine that in the example above, the CEO has unfolded the "increase the profitability of the company" Objective to an "increase sales" Objective for the VP Sales. The VP Sales is likely to unfold this Objective equally to all members of his organization who sell or who manage salespeople, such as a regional sales director, a sales supervisor, and ultimately account executives. What will vary between their OKRs is the Key Result attributed to each Objective, which will vary depending on the products sold by the team, sales territories, etc. The example below helps illustrate that:

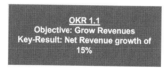

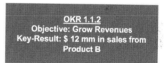

Unfolding the same Objective with different Key-Results

Note that the VP's Objective can be unfolded both as the same Objective for one director and a different Objective for another director. The VP can unfold sales quotas to most of his organization under the same Objective - increase sales -, but simultaneously unfold an "implement Salesforce to all AEs" Project to the Director of Sales Ops and an "expand to new geography XYZ" Project to another director or team who will be in charge of executing it.

Assigning Key Results to Objectives

Once the Objective has been defined, as we illustrated above, the next step is to determine Key Results that can measure and prove if the Objective has been reached.

To facilitate the assignment of Key Results to Objectives, let's use the model we talked about at the beginning of the book:

"We will _ _ _ _ _ _, and we will know if we were successful if we can _ _ _ _ _ _ _ _ _ _ _ _ _ _ _ ."

The first space is filled by your Objective, and the second to the fourth are filled by the Key Results.
Let's use the example of profitability again to illustrate our definition:

- **Objective**: Increase the profitability of the company
- **Key-Result 1**: Reach a net profit margin of 10%
- **Key-Result 2**: increase net profit to $12 million

If we fill in the gaps above, we get:

"We will *increase the profitability of the company*, and we will know if we were successful if we *reach a net profit margin of 10%*, and *increase net profit to $12 million.*"

Now you have a clear Key Result that allows the entire company to know, in an undisputed way, whether the Objective of "increasing the company's profitability" has been reached.

Please note that I've also coupled two different Key Results to the same Objective. That's one of the beauties of having OKRs. These two Key Results balance each other out, and we use them in this way to avoid weird behavior. For example, the company could reach the profit dollar amount Key Result by compromising margins (by handing out excessive discounts,) or reach the margin Key Result by compromising the dollar amount of revenues (by increasing prices and thus reducing quantities).

Choosing the right KPIs for your Key Results

Good Key Results have some features that make the process easier and more effective.

First, the Key Result needs to be based on a quantitative indicator, or KPI. Good Key Results are based on "plottable" indicators such as "sales of product X," "Y to Z conversion rate on the website," "employee turnover at office W," etc.

Several companies make the mistake of creating fuzzy Key Results because there's little clarity on which KPI is used. "Sales," for example, is a terrible KPI because it tells the organization very little about the specifics of how the KPI will actually be measured. It's better to use "revenues from new orders" or "net revenues for the company."

Some companies go beyond and require people to use pre-determined KPIs calculated by a central authority like a Business Intelligence team. We think that's too much. You'll be fine if people just clarify the right KPI to measure in the Key Result, and maybe even write down the formula for how to calculate the KPI in the Key Result description.

Second, ideally, this KPI is easy to measure. Monitoring, which we'll cover in a bit, can be harmed by Key Results and their KPIs being too hard to measure, which causes people not to track them enough, or at all. Therefore, easy-to-measure KPIs are always better than hard-to-measure ones.

Third, it's important that the indicator be sensitive to the efforts of the OKR's "owner." There's little use in basing an OKR on KPIs that are out of their owner's control. People have to have authority and autonomy to influence their

OKRs. In addition, KPIs need to be measurable in a cadence that's contained within the short cycle. There's no point, of course, in basing a quarterly OKR on yearly sales, or usage of a product that's not going to be released within the cycle.

How far should you unfold OKRs?

According to Vicente Falconi, whom we've already quoted much here, "unfolding will only be complete when all goals result in plans of action that are, in fact, the most important parts of planning." Company OKRs have to be unfolded until they've become action plans and projects to be executed by someone or some team somewhere.

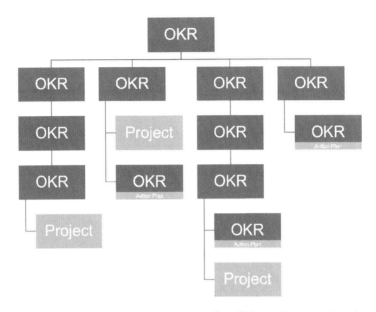

The "End of the Line": All OKRs must "end" in Projects and Action Plans

We briefly talked about Action Plans and Projects above. The difference between the two lies in the complexity of the initiative: An Action Plan tends to be simpler (a set of tasks), and a Project tends to be more complex, including longer deadlines and eventually more than one "owner."

Action plans

Every Objective has to either be unfolded, in which case it becomes another Objective or a Project, or generate an Action Plan.

To create a good action plan, the OKR owner should start by analyzing the situation at hand – that is, the reality surrounding the OKR to be achieved. After the analysis is done, possible areas of attack are listed and then prioritized according to their impact on the OKR and their cost, which is gauged by complexity.

Solutions are then discovered with techniques such as five whys, the fishbone diagram, design thinking, and brainstorming. This is followed by developing possible corrective and preventive solutions to the problem.

With those areas of attack prioritized, the OKR owner can then establish an Action Plan that summarizes when, where, why, by whom, and for how much these actions will be executed.

Who should have individual OKRs?

This is a very controversial subject. Some OKR coaches, such as Felipe Castro, founder of Lean Performance, argue that multi-disciplinary teams should only have team-level OKRs, and therefore members of the team shouldn't have individual OKRs. The reasoning goes, allocating responsibility for results is virtually impossible in these cases. We think that's a fine example where individual OKRs make no sense.

To illustrate that point, let's think of an e-commerce company that has a team (for example, a Scrum or a squad made up of designers, engineers, and product managers) whose priority for a given cycle is to reduce the abandonment rates of the shopping cart.

We can think of an obvious Objective for the squad: improve the shopping cart conversion rate. We can also think of some pretty obvious Key Results, like "reduce shopping cart abandonment rate to 5% in this quarter." Would it be possible to further unfold this OKR to individual team members?

Let's fast forward a bit and say the team is successful in reaching the OKR. How much of it can be attributed to the front-end engineers, who have coded the improvements in HTML and CSS? Or to the back-end engineers, who have coded the improvements on the server? Or the designers, who have drawn the screen changes, created mock-ups, and tested them with users for ease of use? Or the product managers, who have managed the entire process, and interfaced with other teams within the company?

As I've implied, multi-disciplinary product teams are great examples of when unfolding individual OKRs makes little sense.

Sales, on the other hand, is an area of the company where

unfolding OKRs to the individuals is almost always a good alternative. That's because salespeople tend to be held accountable for their individual results, which are very easy to measure: an account executive's results are her sales numbers. Therefore, OKRs can be unfolded to them, and Key Results will be based on their production levels.

Everything in between sales and product can be a bit fuzzy.

Generally, the higher up the person is in the organizational chart, the bigger the chance she'll have individual OKRs. As we get farther down the chart, chances are that lower-level employees will be more accountable for executing Projects, which are efforts and must not be confused with OKRs, which are results.

A manager in the accounts payable team, working under the CFO's organization, may have an OKR about reducing the number of errors in both invoices paid and received, and another OKR about reducing days-receivable or extending days-payable. She will then unfold to her team a couple of Projects that she and her team believe will help hit those goals, like implementing a major new piece of software and reengineering the account payables approval process.

Using OKRs in software product teams

Setting OKRs for product teams is a very tough challenge. In 9 out of every 10 OKR implementations we take part in product teams set their OKRs as if they were deliverables. In this chapter, we'll discuss how to use OKRs in software product teams.

OKRs are not about features to be shipped

The big challenge is that OKRs are a tough discipline, and most people get it wrong when trying to use it in product teams. The OKR ecosystem also doesn't help – a quick search over the internet led me to a competitor's website, where I found the following example as inspiration for a good OKR [1]:

> "Objective: Implement new 360-degree product planning process
>
> Key Results:
>
> · Document clear role division between sales, marketing, design and (sic) development
> · Decide on and document the process of input

methods to and from sales, marketing, design and (sic) development back into product management

· Integrate user testing into all activities in product planning and design phase
· Integrate user testing into pre-launch testing phase"

Not to mention Google's re:Work website (Google is, as you might already know, the company that has basically helped the OKR gospel spread throughout Silicon Valley) that cites "eat 5 pies" as an example of a great objective, but I'll leave that for another post (if you want to learn the basics of OKRs, read our book, OKRs, From Mission to Metrics).

Anyway, most product OKRs look something like this:

Objective: Deliver new iOS app

Key results:

· Design first concept
· Code MVP
· Get beta testers
· Publish the app by November on the app stores

What's wrong?

OKRs are all about RESULTS

If you read Inspired, by Marty Kagan, founder of the Silicon Valley Product Group and a big hotshot, you'll get the idea that we should ditch roadmaps as we know them (long lists of features to be built) and replace them with OKRs.

What he's saying is that roadmaps are bad for product teams because they aren't a direction teams can chase. Roadmaps are usually built by a hodgepodge of intuition, hunches, and highest-paid-people-in-the-room opinions.

Instead of a roadmap, leaders should set clear OKRs - or results expected - and let their product teams figure out what to do - or what to build - in order to reach them. But setting proper OKRs is tough, and usually, teams veer back to some sort of mishmash between OKRs and a roadmap. And roadmaps are collections of efforts.

When we ship a new feature, there's no guarantee it will generate any impact on our business, good or bad. Users may not even use them (and we know the hard way that's frequently the case).

So don't confuse efforts and results, roadmaps and, impact: OKRs should be about results and not efforts. Delivering features is an *effort* that will hopefully produce *results* down the line. Let's call features, or the effort product teams put up, "output."

Financials are not good results to aim at

Marvelous. Now we know that OKRs shouldn't look like roadmaps or features to be shipped.

We have to find results with which to work. So what results can a shipped feature produce?

At the highest level, and being rather simplistic, features should produce more revenues or fewer costs for the company that owns the product. That impact on the bottom line can come sooner, such as more conversion for an e-commerce website this quarter, or later, such as more perceived quality on a social network's timeline that will reduce churn and thus produce more revenues in the future.

But these sorts of business results, are really hard to relate to or to optimize for. The impact of features is hard to map to the top line or the bottom line of the company. (Of course, some exceptions must exist: when a team works on fixing terrible bugs on the check-out flow of a website, they may impact sales quite directly, in the form of getting customers to close rather than to go shop elsewhere. But generally, things are a bit more nuanced.)

Another problem is that financials are impacted by too many variables. We can't attribute to the checkout squad how much revenue customers are bringing into an e-commerce operation. It's also a function of the product mix, the overall store usability, shipping costs, and speed, only to name a few. It wouldn't be fair nor helpful.

So we need to find other results to base our OKRs on.

Outcomes

Joshua Seiden has a great book called "Outcomes over Output" that will help us make progress [2]. It's honestly a must-read for all product teams.

Seiden calls business results, like revenues, profits, and costs, "Impacts" (we'll capitalize the terms he uses when using them to his specification). He also calls the stuff product teams build, or features, "Output."

But Seiden doesn't stop there: he suggests there's something in between Outputs and Impact that we should be aware of: Outcomes. The definition of an Outcome is quite simple: "the human behaviors that drive business results."

He goes on saying that " we want our customers to log onto our site more often, or put an extra item in their shopping cart, or share an interesting article with a friend, or upload a picture, or complete a task in less time. What do all of these things have in common? They're all measures of customer behavior. They might be small changes in a big system, but they are specific, and they allow our teams the flexibility to figure out the most efficient way to solve the problem, to deliver the behavior change that we seek, and to make a meaningful contribution to the impacts (revenue, profitability) that our executive leaders care about."

In our business (software that helps teams implement 1:1s, ongoing feedback, and peer-to-peer recognition), some examples of Outcomes we build for are:

- Number of feedbacks given by users
- Number of 1:1s done on time by users
- Percentage of users from the "direct report" persona who've gotten feedback in the last 30 days

You get the picture. Outcomes are user behaviors that we believe will drive Impact (or business results). As a rule of thumb, if your OKRs - more specifically, your key results - don't come out of Mixpanel, you're probably doing it wrong.

Outcomes, experiments, and MVPs

You read that right: we believe Outcomes will lead to Impact.
What separates great product teams from mediocre ones
is how often they get those assumptions right, and/or how
quickly they iterate when wrong.

Tying back to Marty Kagan, the fact that Output doesn't
always lead to Outcomes, nor Outcomes to Impact, by the
way, is why product teams should prefer OKRs over a roadmap:
roadmaps should be flexible, and not set in stone, since
they will frequently change in the journey of maximizing
for Impact.
Of course, product teams – or most product teams nowa-
days – will still have some sort of backlog of features to
build. But this backlog won't be simply a refined material-
ization of the roadmap: it will hopefully be a list of features
that have been proven, to the extent possible, to generate
Outcomes.
The process of finding out if features will indeed produce
results is called discovery. Discovery happens via experiments, or the smallest efforts (i.e., time from the team)
that can prove our hypotheses of what features will drive
Outcomes, and what Outcomes will drive Impact. Product
teams should always be running experiments that test

those hypotheses, with the least code possible.

By the way, a product team should work on its discovery efforts in parallel to its delivery efforts. Discovery is finding out which features will lead to Outcomes. Delivery is building these features with production-level quality. The good thing is that Outcomes, on which your OKRs should be based, change with much less frequency. They tend to be metrics we'll optimize on the mid to long-run. It's hard to think of Facebook not maximizing the time users spend scrolling on their News Feeds [3], or the number of posts a user likes at a given active session.

Setting OKRs with Outcomes

Ok. Enough with the product-speak. So what does a proper OKR look like for a product team?

Let's say we have a product team at Qulture.Rocks [4] composed of a product manager, a designer, and a few front-and-back-end engineers. Let's also say that Qulture.Rocks' OKRs this quarter revolve around growing MRR from new customers, growing MRR from existing customers (via net expansion), and burning less than a given amount of cash each month, in order to preserve runway. Their objective [5] could look like the following:

Increase the activation rate of technical leaders
with our product

Where did this objective come from?

Members of the executive team have found out that leaders
in tech teams are a great persona to optimize for: they
convert at a low cost (CAC,) and churn very little when
properly activated (the process that starts with a sign-up
and ends with a happy, active, and retained user). They've
also found that they aren't very successful in activating
technical leaders: more than 50% of those who sign up end
up abandoning the product before experiencing its value.

Ok. Now, what key results [6] does the team have?

Key result: Net activation rate of users classified as "tech
leads" from 50% to 70%

What's cool about this OKR is that our product team can
run a great number of experiments of things they could
do to improve our activation rate. They could create an
onboarding flow that's specific to tech leads; they could
call each tech lead on the phone to explain the value of the
product to them; they could pre-load the application with
product team OKRs so that tech leads quickly see value; or
they could work on an email campaign to get these users
back on the product (resurrect them).

Since OKRs should be aligned up (or unfolded down, what-ever you prefer,) this OKR can be aligned - or contribute - to the following OKR:

Objective: Improve our customer retention

Key result: Gross monthly churn rate, from 2% to 1.4%

And this "churn" OKR can be aligned to the following company-wide OKR:

Objective: Improve our MRR in line with the best in the business

Key result: MRR, from $ 240k to $ 330k

But what if we already have a roadmap?

Most probably, if you're reading this article you already have a roadmap. So I want to make clear you don't have to chop your roadmap into pieces right away, even though that would be neat.

What you can do is look at what's next in your roadmap. Ask yourself what Outcomes do we want to create with this Output (feature)? And then what Impact do we want to create in the business with this Outcome? These questions will allow you to first set the right frame of mind and, second, check if your roadmap makes business sense. Then you should gradually stop updating your roadmap and setting OKRs instead.

A big challenge: enterprise software

Last, let's talk about some challenges enterprise product teams may face in this journey of using OKRs to change from Output to Outcomes to Impact.

Getting this right in enterprise software is the hardest for two reasons: the connection of Outcomes and Impacts may be weak or hard to prove, and/or Outcomes may be hard to properly measure. This is true because, respectively, in enterprise software, buyers rarely use the product (check out this tweet), and usage is usually affected by extraneous factors.

To explain the first case, let's imagine Jane the CFO works for Jalmart (fictional characters, please). She buys Oriple ERP because she wants to have all her financial information organized in one place (her employer is getting ready for an IPO.) Now let's move to a product team within Oriple's New Dehli offices, that takes care of a specific feature that handles payable invoices. Let's also say this team wants to improve the rate of invoices properly input on the system within the same active session. If they do this, accounts payable analysts within the companies that use Oriple will probably love how easy it has become to do that workflow. But will that really affect Oriple's revenues? Or its churn rate? Jane the CFO will probably never even see that feature. And it will take A LOT of kicking and screaming from the whole company to get her to switch ERPs, especially after the nightmarish implementation process that Agzzenture ran for two years.

In these cases, the assumption around if an Outcome will generate Impact is hard to test. Product teams will have to rely on their intuition (and market trends that point to the consumerization of enterprise IT) to get work done.

To explain the second case, let's imagine Ned the Analyst. He "uses" Facelook Wordplace because Jowen and Co's HR department implemented the corporate social network company-wide. "Uses" is in quotes because Ned rarely logs in. He thinks it is a nuisance. Come next month the company's CEO, Gretta, announces she's resigning in a weird Wordplace post, and everybody single employee in the company logs in to read it and gossip about it.

Now let's cut to a growth team within Facelook that handles Wordplace, a young product with about 15 customers. They have an OKR that revolves around resurrecting inactive users and are running several experiments around email campaigns and push notifications. The team thought it had some promising A/B test results on the push front and were about to scope a full-blown feature for the back-log when they learned about the post at Jowen. They'll either have to scrap the OKR altogether and move forward by sheer faith, or stop everything they're doing and wait for more test results.

There's no right answer to this question.

You might think this is uncommon, but there are many enterprise products that have usage metrics polluted by "offline" behaviors, and it can be very hard to clean the metrics and get something meaningful. HR software is especially tricky, as we can attest.

Notes

[1] Maybe they should change their business to SEO con-sulting ;)

[2] Like we frequently do at Qulture.Rocks, we've pur-chased five copies of the book for our product team to share.

[3] It takes a "time well spent" movement to change that.

[4] We do have one exactly like that.

[5] Let's remember: an objective is a qualitative goal, usu-ally starting with a verb and ending with a non-numerical description of an aspect of the business to be improved.

Some examples: "increase adoption," "reduce our cash burn," or "enhance our customer satisfaction."

[6] Let's also remember: a key result is the sum of a KPI (e.g., "net profit of the company in 2020"), a base level ("100.000") and a target level ("200.000".) We believe objectives should be narrow enough in scope to carry one or two key results at most. If your objective has more than two key results, you've probably too big a scope.

9. Monitoring

More important than the definition of OKRs are the rituals that form their cadence: what we'll call monitoring. Monitoring is where the rubber meets the road. It's where the benefits of OKRs (performance, excellence, alignment, and learning) come to life and produce better results across the enterprise.

Results meetings

The first and most important part of monitoring OKRs is
the Results Meetings.

Results meetings are cadenced gatherings where a leader
will meet with her direct reports to discuss their OKRs and
Projects.

The meeting agenda is incredibly simple: Every direct report has an allotment of time where she presents *which*
OKRs and Projects on her panel are off-track, then explains
why these OKRs and Projects are off-track, and, finally,
enumerates the actions she's *already taken* to get them
back on track. Summing it up, every participant states:

- Which OKRs/Projects are off-track
- Why these OKRs/Projects are off-track, and
- Which actions are already underway to get these OKRs/Pro-
  jects back on track

Why focus only on what's off-track? Because time is extremely limited, and meetings can quickly become long
and boring. Therefore the focus is exclusively on what's
"red."

Fostering the right culture

A big part of making monitoring, and OKRs in general, work is to foster a constructive, positive environment around these meetings.

It's of the utmost importance that those employees who present what's off-track aren't condemned or humiliated in public. The idea isn't to scold people in front of their peers but to solve real problems and think.

The idea is that there's nothing wrong with making mistakes - that is, forming hypotheses of how you're going to hit your OKRs that don't work out. The only problem is if people make commitments, like action plans, and don't follow through with them. That sort of problem should be handled offline like any other behavioral issue.

We can attest to the fact that when people honor their commitments, even not hitting OKRs feels constructive and productive, because Results Meetings tend to be intellectually challenging and interesting. People are honestly trying to figure out what was wrong with their reasoning and what they'll do differently to get OKRs and Projects back on-track.

A great framework for assessing progress

In order to create a culture of learning and problem solving (as opposed to a culture of guilt and finger-pointing), we seek inspiration in how Vicente Falconi (2012) suggests goal attainment be analyzed.

He describes a two-by-two matrix that has, on the one side, if the action plan was executed or not, and on the other if the OKR was achieved or not.

With it, we are able to analyze whether an OKR has been achieved "on purpose" or "by chance," and the same for OKRs that were not achieved (remember, on-track OKRs won't be discussed in Results Meetings unless there's a lot of time to be spared).

- **Quadrant 1 – actions were executed according to plan, but the OKR is off-track**: In this case, the hypothesis, and thus the action plan, were wrong. The team has to find out why the plan was wrong in the first place and adjust it.
- **Quadrant 2 – actions weren't executed according to plan, and the OKR is on-track**: Here, the main focus of the meeting should be on what caused the OKR to be on-track even though the plan wasn't executed. It's great that the OKR is on-track, but the team should understand exactly what factors weren't

factored in in the first place. Of course, it's also important to understand why the plan wasn't executed. If there were reasonable exogenous factors that prevented the plan from being executed, the team must understand why they were not neutralized with new actions or alternative courses of action. Of course, sometimes a lack of execution just means a behavioral problem, which should be addressed one-on-one by the manager.

- **Quadrant 3 – actions were executed according to plan, and the OKR is on-track**: Even when OKRs are on-track, teams must carefully reflect on their achievements and assess whether they're a consequence of the action plan or of exogenous factors. What factors were these? Why were they not foreseen? The team must understand the whys behind each response.

- **Quadrant 4 – actions were not executed according to plan, and OKR is off-track**: This one is the easiest. The solution is just to get back to executing the plan and to figure out why the plan was not carried out in the first place. The manager should also figure out, as discussed in Quadrant 2, why the plan wasn't executed and treat possible behavioral issues one-on-one accordingly.

Now let's talk a bit about some tools that can help you figure out why things are off-track prior to Results Meetings.

Five Whys

The "five whys" is a very simple method to get to the root cause of a problem. When people get on the first layer of a problem (the first "why"), they tend to only scratch the surface of the problem. Therefore, the tool suggests asking "why" to a problem as many times as necessary (five is just a placeholder) until the ultimate root cause is encountered.

A simple example can illustrate how "five whys" works:

> Question: Sales fell by 10%. Why?
> Answer: Because of the demonstrations that took place in the city.
> Q: Why did the demonstrations affect sales?
> A: Because some streets were closed, and our trucks couldn't reach the merchants.
> Q: Why couldn't our trucks reach merchants?
> A: Because the only open streets were narrow, where our trucks couldn't pass.
> Q: Why weren't smaller trucks used to deliver goods on that day?
> A: Because we don't own smaller trucks.

Boom! You've reached the root cause of the sales down-turn, which is far more subtle and specific than simply blaming the demonstrations.

Great root-cause analysis makes planning easy. In this case, the suggestion is to lease smaller trucks to be used during the rallies planned for the next month. If sales keep up after the experiment, the company then adopts a new standard: to arrange for a fleet of smaller trucks to be on call for such unforeseen events.

10. Debriefing

Debriefing is where the OKR cycle ends, and a new cycle starts. Its main purpose is to wrap up the scoring of the OKRs and to learn from what happened throughout the cycle.

Grading OKRs

There's a lot of discussion around how OKRs should be graded (or scored, or rated – these should all be used as synonyms) at the end of the cycle. Google's approach is to keep it incredibly simple, so there are only five possible achievement scores for an OKR:

- 0.0: No progress made
- 0.3: Little progress made (something achievable with minimal effort)
- 0.5: Reasonable progress (something achievable with considerable effort)
- 0.7: Expected progress (which is achievable with the expected effort; as we discussed earlier, 0.7, or 70%, is "100%" at Google)
- 1.0: Extraordinary progress (more than expected)

Google encourages its employees to preset what these scores represent (in terms of actual results) at the start of the cycle. For example, a team that sets an OKR of "reduce page load times on Google search by 10%" may agree upfront with its leadership that a decrease lower than 2% will mean 0.0, or no progress made; they may also agree that a decrease from 2,01% to 5% will mean 0.3, or little progress made, and so on, and so forth. The important part of setting the grading "ruler" upfront is to minimize the amount of energy dispended on grading the OKR at the end of the cycle.

At other companies, other grading scales are used. They can vary from simple 1-to-5 ratings, letters or even percentages that exceed 100% (a level comparable to Google's "extraordinary progress"). Let's call these the subjective rating way of grading Key Results.

Rating scales don't have to be the only way to score OKRs. Another way to score them is based on the actual progress that's been made on the underlying KPIs. If a Key Result was to reduce customer turnover from 10% per month to 5% per month, and actual turnover was 5%, 100% of this Key Result was achieved (of course, if the turnover at the end of the cycle was 10%, 0% progress was achieved, and so on). Let's call this the linear mathematical way of grading Key Results.

Some Key Results can have binary achievements, such as an M&A deal: It was either completed or not completed. But this type of Key Result should be the exception and not the rule.

If you are investing in a high-performance, results-oriented culture, tracking the KPIs on which Key Results are set is a must. It will make everything easier and more objective.

Running the debriefing

During the debriefing part of the cycle, the company finalizes its OKRs by inputting the last data on KPIs and getting final achievements. If the monitoring phase was well-done, this will be very easy and fast.

The next phase is having people debrief on what went right and wrong. For each OKR, we suggest everybody presents a simple reflection:

- Where the results achieved (yes/no)? What went right and what went wrong?
- Why did these things go right or wrong?
- What have I learned from this cycle that I'll take with me and the company?

This can be a simple form to be filled in a performance management application or a couple of slides to be presented to the team (or both). What's important is that those presenting their debriefings are honest and self-reflective about their performance and their learnings. That's really what the process is all about.

At Google, senior management presents a debriefing of organizational OKRs every quarter in an all-hands meeting that follows the company's board of directors meeting.

11. Most common mistakes

Implementing OKRs can fail for a number of reasons. Here we'll detail the main ones:

Not doing it gradually

OKRs should be implemented gradually:

- From fewer OKRs towards more OKRs
- From company goals towards individual goals
- From shorter iteration cycles (and faster course-correction) towards longer iteration cycles

If you try many things at once, such as unfolding five company OKRs down to the individual level in an annual cycle, your project will surely fail. People won't know what the hell is going on, they won't remember their OKRs, teams won't monitor their OKRs, etc. It's very important that the company starts at the appropriate cadence, and that means to warm the engines gradually, to do rituals like results meetings right, so as to create healthy habits.

Baby steps: You can start with one company-wide Objective and three or four Key Results in a one-month cycle. See how it goes, learn from the process, and repeat. After three months, unfold the OKRs loosely to the teams. Three more monthly cycles. And so on. If the company has incorporated the cadence – the habit – of monitoring its OKRs, you've already made tremendous progress towards more alignment and results-orientation

Setting too many OKRs

One of the great advantages of OKRs, especially for companies that do nothing strategic planning or goal-setting, is that they lead to greater focus. As the OKR cycles are shorter, you can afford to have a narrower focus per cycle, aligning the entire organization on the most pressing issues.

The total number of Objectives of any single entity (be it the company, a team, or a person) should not exceed the fingers on one hand (three is best). More than that, and they won't be remembered.

Let's look at a practical example of a product manager's OKRs for the first quarter of 2016:

- **Objective 1**: Improve engagement on the SaaS product
- **Key Results**: Increase the number of monthly active users by 15%; Increase the average time spent on each page by 5%

- **Objective 2**: Generate a high level of customer satisfaction
- **Key Result**: NPS> 8 with> 90% of customer responses

- **Objective 3**: Launch new reconciliation feature
- **Key Result**: Usage of at least four customers per day; Ten (upsell) paying users.

As you can see, the PM has three things he has to focus on this quarter:

- Engagement
- Customer satisfaction
- New reconciliation feature

These priorities are supported by four Key Results that support them. This is highly manageable and easy to remember. As Marcel Telles, former CEO of AmBev (now SAB Miller + Anheuser-Busch InBev), says: "Goals have to fit on the fingers of one hand."

"Setting and forgetting"

Goals lose their *raison d'être* if they aren't monitored. Accountability is critical: Employees must own their OKRs, and Key Results should be monitored on an ongoing basis. There are a number of reasons for this:

- In discussing the whys of each goal, the organization learns what works and what doesn't work. What advantage is there in knowing that someone has achieved their OKRs if he or she doesn't know which specific course of action has led to the results achieved?
- Constant monitoring shows that the organization cares about OKRs. Many companies spend time and effort deploying and discussing OKRs, only to forget them until the end of the cycle. If the company isn't monitoring its OKRs, then individual contributors, teams, and leaders won't monitor their OKRs. It's an example that has to be set by the company from top to bottom.

Company OKRs must be monitored at all-hands meetings; team OKRs should be monitored at special Results team meetings. Never skip a Results Meeting: just as zero-tolerance helped end New York City violence, it will do wonders for its high-performance culture.

OKRs that are too hard

There is scientific evidence (Locke, 2011) that difficult goals create better performance. That's why we talk so much about *stretch goals*. Carlos Britto, CEO of AB InBev, says the ideal goals should be those "you know 80% how to beat. The other 20% will be learned along the way." But science also suggests that Goals must be attainable, meaning that they're realistic: Setting goals that are too difficult frustrates people (who have to believe they can achieve them for the methodology to be effective).

Locke and Latham say, once again:

"Nothing generates success as success. On the other hand, nothing generates feelings of despair like a constant failure. The main purpose of goal setting is to increase the individual's level of motivation, but goals can have exactly the opposite effect. Consequently, the supervisor should be looking for unrealistic goals, and be prepared to change them when necessary."

Starting with moonshots

One of the most common mistakes made by companies that are adopting OKRs for the first time is to focus on stretch goals in the beginning.

When companies start using OKRs, employees usually don't have a very good understanding of how its main KPI has behaved in the past. Because of that ignorance, they usually set very aggressive Key Results, for fear that they will not be too challenging. That fear can be compounded by reading stuff about "roof shots," "moonshots," and other Google fancy practices at Google (which, as we've seen, aren't that real).

Needless to say, if no one achieves their OKRs, the first impression left by OKRs is terrible; the image of the OKRs is tarnished, and people start to think that not achieving their OKRs is the rule - or worse - they completely abandon them.

The right way to do this is to set conservative OKRs to begin with: levels that aren't a big stretch. After a few cycles of consistency and commitment, the company can slowly start stretching its goals.

After more maturity is achieved (where the company as a whole reaches 70-80% of targets, people can start having the freedom to set one stretch OKR per cycle, but not more than that.

Goals that are too easy

Alternatively, OKRs can't be too easy. Research indicates that very easy goals generate low levels of motivation and energy due to their lack of challenge in the eyes of their owners. According to Locke: "One of the most consistent findings of the level of difficulty of the goals is that when goals are very low, people often achieve them, but subsequent levels of motivation and energy typically fall precipitously, and goals are narrowly missed." In other words, people adjust their efforts to minimize their energy expenditure.

12. Bibliography

Akao, Yoji. "Hoshin Kanri: Policy Deployment for Successful TQM". Productivity Press, 2004.

Ariely, Dan, and Matt R. Trower. "Payoff: The Hidden Logic That Shapes Our Motivations". TED Books, 2016.

Babich, Pete, & Ragazzo, Ernest. "Hoshin Handbook". Total Quality Engineering, 1998.

Bechtell, Michele L. "The Management Compass: Steering the Corporation Using Hoshin Planning". Blackhall, 2002.

Bock, Laszlo. "Work Rules!: Insights from Inside Google That Will Transform How You Live and Lead". Grand Central Publishing, 2017.

Carson, P. P., Carson, K. D., & Headya, R. B. (1994). "Cecil alec mace: The man who discovered goal-setting". International Journal of Public Administration, 17(9), 1679–1708. doi:10.1080/01 900699408524960

Doerr, John. "Measure What Matters How Google, Bono, and the Gates Foundation Rock the World with OKRs".

Portfolio/Penguin, 2018.

Doran, G. T. (1981). "There's a S.M.A.R.T. way to write management's goals and objectives". Management Review. AMA FORUM. 70 (11): 35–36.

Drucker, Peter F. (2010). "The Practice of Management". Harper Collins e-books.

Grant, Anthony M. (September 2012). "An integrated model of goal-focused coaching: an evidence-based framework for teaching and practice" (PDF). International Coaching Psychology Review. 7 (2): 146–165 (149). Archived from the original (PDF) on 2014-11-29.

Grove, A. S. "High Output Management". Souvenir Press, 1983.

LaFollette, W. R., & Fleming, R. J. (1977). "The Historical Antecedents of Management by Objective". Academy of Management Proceedings, 1977(1).

Levinson, Harry (2003). "Management by Whose Objectives?". Harvard Business Review. Retrieved from https://hbr.org in December 5th, 2018.

Locke, Edwin A. (2001). "Motivation by goal setting". In Golembiewski, Robert T. Handbook of organizational behavior(2nd ed.).

Locke, Edwin A. (May 1968). "Toward a theory of task motivation and incentives". Organizational Behavior and Human Performance.

Locke, Edwin A.; Latham, Gary P. (October 2006). "New directions in goal-setting theory" (PDF). Current Directions in Psychological Science.

McGregor, Douglas (1972). "An Uneasy Look at Performance Appraisal". Harvard Business Review. Retrieved from https://hbr.org in December 5th, 2018.

Odiorne, George S. Management by Objectives: a System of Managerial Leadership. Pitman, 1974.

Pink, Daniel H. "Drive: The Surprising Truth About What Motivates Us". Canongate Books, 2018.

Acknowledgements

I'd like to thank all the authors I've cited on the book: I am standing on the shoulders of brilliant giants. My family – Danielle, Lia, Eureka, and Eugenia – for all love and support, as well as pacience with my long working hours and frequent travels. All the Q-Players that work with me in realizing our mission of empowering companies to achieve great things: we all served as lab rats in learning more about OKRs at work. Working with you all honors and humbles me on a daily basis. Ali Rowghani, whose amazing article, *The Second Job of a Startup CEO*, opened up my eyes about the importance of having all employees aligned, from mission to metrics. Our investors at Qulture.Rocks, who fuel our endeavors. Of course, this list is not exhaustive, and I've certainly forgotten many worthy mentions.

Final note

We've finally reached the end of this incredible OKRs journey! I hope you've enjoyed the content and now feel more comfortable with implementing OKRs at your organization.

This book is a constantly evolving piece of work, so there's a chance you don't have the most up-to-date version at your fingertips. Check-out http://qulture.rocks to download the latest version.

To implement OKRs, you may need some even more tactical tips on how to conduct the workshops, dynamics, and meetings throughout the cycle, and whose workings we describe only at at a high-level in this book. To learn more about it all, please reach out to me and our team at growth@qulturerocks.com.

Cheers,

Francisco

Made in the USA
Columbia, SC
11 July 2023

20266750R00088